Bubbe, Mimi & Gigi:

Grandmother Name Book *EVER*

Cathy Caputo Livingstone

Livingstone, Cathy Caputo
Bubbe, Gigi & Mimi: The Best Grandmother Name Book Ever.
Written and researched by Cathy Caputo Livingstone
Grandmother Character Art: Cathy Swett, Glen Ridge, NJ
Book Letters & Swirly Designs: Cathy and Kelly Ann Livingstone
Cover Design and Interior Design: Kim Gledhill, www.kimgledhill.com
Editor: Gretchen Kunzler Doner

Published by Oxford Street Publishing

Printed in the Unites States of America
ISBN: 978-0-615-43428-5

Dedications

First, to my mother "Bubbe," for her unwavering and steadfast determination to claim her rightful grandmother name.

To my family, Glenn, Kelly Ann and Will, who lived through mounds of papers everywhere and hours of seemingly endless writing and editing. Without their love, support and understanding, I would have never completed this book.

To my fun, adventurous friend Cathy Swett whose incredible artistry and talent I owe the fabulous grandma caricatures.

To my neighbor and literary expert, Nancy Perlman, who unselfishly gave of her time to guide me through this complicated literary process.

To every friend and friend-of-friend, who took the time to tell me their wonderful grandmother names and stories. It is because of your generosity this book is true and authentic.

Lastly, to everyone who ever asked me, "How's your book coming along?" It truly inspired and encouraged me to keep going and greatly motivated me to finish this project. For that and more, I am so grateful.

Contents

Foreword

Bubbe, my Irish Catholic mother, unknowingly initiated the idea for this book. When our daughter was born, my mother announced that she would not be called "Grandma" by her grandchildren, but "Bubbe." My siblings and I thought it was quite comical, since Bubbe is a traditional Jewish grandmother name and we are Catholic. However, the name actually seemed fitting, even though we didn't know the true definition of the name "Bubbe." Notwithstanding any criticism or input from us, my mother prevailed and "Bubbe Caputo" was born.

Introduction

No two grandmothers are alike. Therefore, why not a helpful book to assist you in choosing the best name for you? Today's grandmothers are women-on-the-go and are playing a significant role in their grandchildren's lives every day. It is important that your "Grandmother" name defines the unique, wonderful grandmother that you are.

The following grandmother name "descriptions" were derived from many sources: various grandmother stories people shared with me, online grandparent blogs and my imagination and interpretation of existing grandmothers. Hence, every grandmother name is subject to your creativity, perception and real-life experiences.

Whether you are already a grandmother or a grandmother-to-be, many congratulations to you! May this book bring you some laughs and fun moments with your family and friends. Best wishes for a joyous and adventurous Grandmotherhood!

"When a child is born, so are grandmothers."

—Judith Levy, Author

PART I

Grandma Name Quiz

Congratulations on your upcoming "Grandmotherhood" journey! Your first exciting step is choosing your special new Grandma name. Your Grandma name is important because you are unique and special—there's only one you! This Quiz will start you on your way to finding the perfect name for you.

1) Do you drive a _____?:

a) Convertible or Sports Car
b) SUV or Station Wagon
c) Hybrid
d) Cadillac, Buick or 4-door Sedan

2) In your leisure time, you usually _____?:

a) Run marathons, do yoga or rock climb
b) Shop for clothes
c) Volunteer at a local hospital
d) Knit, sew or read a book

3) Your best friend would say your best quality is _____?:

a) Sense of humor
b) Sense of style
c) Sense of smell
d) Sense of direction

4) What is your favorite vacation _____?

a) Downhill skiing in the Rockies
b) Sunning yourself at the beach
c) Camping in the middle of nowhere
d) Wine tasting in Europe

5) Your everyday dress style is mostly _____?:

a) Jeans or sporty clothes
b) Dressy or professional
c) Vintage or "gently worn"
d) Comfy sweats or clothes with elastic waists

6) You last saw a movie in the movie theatre _____?:

a) Last week
b) Last year
c) Not this decade
d) With first boyfriend

7) Your favorite shoes are _____?:

a) Sneakers
b) High heels hot off the runway
c) Flip flops
d) Easy Spirit shoes

8) At an amusement park, you would _____?:

a) Skip the rides and go directly to the karaoke
b) Ride the ferris wheel – because you like to be up high
c) Shoot the ducks for a prize
d) Enjoy the carousel ride only

9) Who would play you in the movie of your life _____?:

a) Raquel Welsh
b) Martha Stewart
c) Whoopi Goldberg
d) Barbara Bush

10) Your favorite kind of house pet is _____?:

a) Dog or cat
b) Parakeet
c) Chia Pet
d) Goldfish

11) For Halloween, you like to dress up as _____?:

a) Witch
b) Playboy Bunny
c) Garage Mechanic
d) Gypsy

12) If you were in a music competition, what song would you sing _____?:

a) "Over the Rainbow"
b) "Born in the USA"
c) "YMCA" or "Hokie-Pokie"
d) "I Can't Get No Satisfaction"

Answers

Mostly A

You are very social, outgoing and are a born leader. Possible Grandmother names for you are: Mimi, Gigi, Dede, Bibi or Glamma.

Mostly B

You are active, adventurous and enjoy the outdoors. Possible Grandmother names for you are: Birdie, Coco, Bubbe, Galini or Vovo.

Mostly C

You are a comedian who loves telling stories and cheering people up. Possible Grandmother names for you are: Manita, Snookie, DaMa, Sassy or Toot.

Mostly D

You are serious, trustworthy and a peacemaker amongst friends and family. Possible Grandmother names for you are: Nana, Gram, Lilly, Nonna or Vela.

PART II

The Best
Grandmother
Names

Abuela (pronounced ä-bā-lä). Literally translated as an old woman grandmother. After a meal at Abuela's house, you are guaranteed to gain a pound or two!

Persona: Always-Cooking Spanish Grandma

Fun Fact: Spanish Saying: "No tiene Abuela?"
Literally translated as "Have you no Grandmother?" Loosely translated as "Have you no conscience, no shame?"

Abuelita (pronounced ä-bā-lē-tä). Little gold earrings adorn this grandma. She has a lot to say and speaks quickly, so pay close attention.

Persona: Fast-Talking Spanish Grandma

Fun Fact: Sara Garcia, movie star of the 1940s and 50s, is affectionately known as Mexico's Abuelita. Garcia's image appears on the label of Mexico's traditional Abuelita chocolate, which is now owned by Nestle.

Abbey (pronounced â-bē). In her house, she subscribes to the "Church of Abbey."

Persona: Holier-than-Thou Grandma

Airy (pronounced â-rē). Literally translated as graceful, fairylike and mannered. Airy has an easy, breezy personality.

Persona: Easy-Going Grandma

"You are never too old to become younger."

—Mae West, Actress

Ajax

(pronounced ā-jăks). Literally translated as having abundant strength and courage. She has always been a workhorse.

Persona: Good-Work-Ethic Grandma

Aja

(pronounced ä-jä). Colorful, flowing fabrics drape Aja. Children marvel at her nose ring.

Persona: Coast-of-India Grandma

Apple

(pronounced ăp-əl). "You are the apple of my eyes," "As American as apple pie."

Persona: Sweet-n-Tart Grandma

Auntie

(pronounced än-tē). Auntie suggests she is way too young to possibly be a grandmother.

Persona: In-Denial Grandma

Austen

(pronounced ä-stən). She is majestic and venerable.

Persona: Romantic Grandma

Fun Fact: Jane Austen (1775-1817) was an English novelist. Her works of romantic fiction are well-known. She is known today as the "Grandma of Chick Lit."

Famous Grandma

**Actress Julie Andrews
is
Grand Julie**

9

B

Baachan
(pronounced bă-chän). Literally translated as "Old Lady."

Persona: Graceful Japanese Grandma

Baba
(pronounced bă-bă). Resembling a former heavyweight champion, Baba is a strong woman who tackles problems head-on.

Persona: Headstrong Serbian Grandma

Fun Fact: Grandmother Witch "Baba Yaga" is a mythical creature in Russian folklore stories who appears both as a warning to kids to be good and as a source of wisdom.

Babcia
(pronounced băb-sē-ä). An outdoorsy woman with a garden everyone envies, she has the gift of making things grow.

Persona: Green-Thumb Polish Grandma

Babka
(pronounced băb-kä). Babka cooks from recipes handed down from generation-to-generation. She will never divulge that secret ingredient!

Persona: Tight-Lipped Polish Grandma

Fun Fact: Babka, a Polish sweet bread, supposedly got its name because its shape is similar to a grandmother—smaller at the top and wider at the bottom.

FUN FACT:
The #1 child care provider today
is Grandparents.

Bana (pronounced bă-nă). Conservative and plain-looking, she has been recycling for years.

Persona: Environmentally-Friendly Grandma

BeBop (pronounced bē-bop). 1. A jazz style that was developed in the 1940s. 2. BeBop is never without her sneakers. Athletic and spry, she easily keeps up with her grandkids.

Persona: In-Shape Grandma

Bebe (pronounced bə-bə). Literally translated as "Baby."

Persona: Sexy-Young-Looking Grandma

Fun Fact: Tony Award winner, Bebe Neuwirth, gained popularity with her portrayal as Dr. Lilith Crane on the hit comedy series, *Cheers*.

BeeBee (pronounced bē-bē). BeeBee likes big, straw hats and is someone who rarely complains.

Persona: No-Worries Grandma

Beanie (pronounced bē-nē). 1. A small, petite hat. 2. A southern belle who is a gracious social butterfly.

Persona: Southern-Plantation Grandma

Beeta (pronounced bē-tä). She is not one to scream and to shy away from bugs and insects. Nature is her passion.

Persona: Outdoors Grandma

Bella

(pronounced bĕl-lä). Just like her name, Bella is a beautiful grandmother. Just a bit of rouge and a hint of lipstick is all she needs.

Persona: Rosy-Cheeks Italian Grandma

Fun Fact: The name, Bella Donna, is translated as "Beautiful Lady." However, the plant with the same name is known as Deadly Nightshade.

Belle Mère

(pronounced bĕl-mər). Literally translated as "Mother-in-Law." Belle Mère exudes charm, sophistication and intelligence.

Persona: Charming French Grandma

Beta

(pronounced bĕ-tä). Literally translated as a measure of volatility. Beta is always willing to jump in and "test the waters."

Persona: Do-as-I-Say-Not-as-I-Do Grandma

Bibi

(pronounced bĭb-bē). Literally translated as alive. Bibi is a cute grandmother with a big personality who enjoys outings in the city with her grandkids.

Persona: Bright-Lights-Big-City Grandma

Fun Fact: Actress Bibi Besch's famous role was as Dr. Carol Marcus, mother of Captain Kirk's son in Star Trek II.

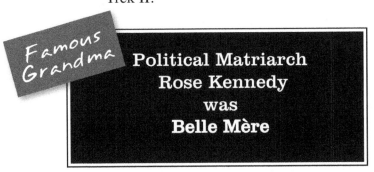

Famous Grandma

**Political Matriarch
Rose Kennedy
was
Belle Mère**

Big Gram

(pronounced bĭg grăm). Old fashioned and down-to-earth. Comfort food, particularly meatloaf and mashed potatoes, is her specialty.

Persona: Homemaker Grandma

Big Mama

(pronounced bĭg mä-mä). A solid, larger-than-life matriarch who can be quite outspoken and somewhat overbearing.

Persona: Speak-When-Spoken-To Urban Grandma

Bink

(pronounced bingk). Bink installed an outdoor pool, so her grandchildren would insist on going over to Grandma Bink's house.

Persona: Spare-the-Rod, Spoil-the-Grandchild Grandma

Binky

(pronounced bingk-ē). An eternal optimist. "Every day is a new day" is her motto.

Persona: Glass-is-Half-Full Grandma

Celebrity Grandma Story:

NBC'S *Today* Show (5/25/11), aired a segment entitled, "Don't call me Grandma! What to call the modern Granny?" The segment featured famous guest grandmas who refuse to go by the moniker, "Grandma."

NYC Real Estate Mogul Barbara Corcoran is
Glam-ma
• • • •
Famous Media Psychologist Dr. Dale Atkins is
Nana

Birdie   (pronounced bŭr-dē). 1. Golf term or small bird. 2. Birdie is someone sporty and "on her game." Preppy pink and lime green clothes are her wardrobe signature.

Persona: The Golf & Tennis Club Grandma

Fun Fact: Bye, Bye Birdie, the 1960 Broadway production, was a Tony Award-winning success.

Bitsy   (pronounced bĭt-sē). Doting, loving and somewhat scatter-brained, she could forget to pick up her grandkids from school due to a tennis match.

Persona: Prep-School Grandma

Bitty   (pronounced bĭt-dē). 1. Tiny, petite. 2. Bitty has had secret credit cards in her name for years.

Persona: Upper-Somewhere Grandma

Bomma   (pronounced bŏm-mä). Bomma likes to wear "festive" holiday sweaters.

Persona: Stay-Out-Of-Her-Way Grandma

Fun Fact: Bomma was a WWII Norwegian freighter vessel.

Bonnie Mamy   (pronounced bŏn-ē-mā-mī). Literally translated as "Good Mother." Bonnie Mamy likes to say, "We have quite enough to do weeding our own garden."

Persona: Old-Belgium-Saying Grandma

"If I'd known how wonderful it would be to have grandchildren, I'd have had them first."

—Lois Wyse, Author

Bonnie My   **(pronounced bŏn-ē-mī).** Literally translated as "My Beautiful." Bonnie My is fiercely loyal to her "clan."

Persona: Beautiful Scottish Grandma

Fun Fact: "My Bonnie Lies over the Ocean" is a traditional Scottish folk song which remains popular in Western culture.

Bootsy   **(pronounced bōōt-sē).** To boot = to kick. Behave or else she'll "bootsy" you!

Persona: Kick-Ass Grandma

Booty   **(pronounced bōōt-tē).** 1. A valuable prize or award. 2. Sharp and dependable. She never misses her weekly poker game with her friends.

Persona: Goodfellas Grandma

Bossie   **(pronounced bôs-ē).** Bossie = Bossy.

Persona: Matriarch Grandma

Bree   **(pronounced brē).** Bree can usually be found with an apron around her waist, a measuring cup in one hand and a trowel in the other.

Persona: Martha-Stewart-Wanna-Be Grandma

Celebrity Grandma Story:

When Martha Stewart became a grandma in March of 2011, her daughter announced, "My mother is going to be called 'Martha'...I don't like the term Grandma!"

American Entrepreneur Martha Stewart is **Martha**.

Bubbe

(pronounced bŭh-bē). She is a great source of Yiddish sayings and has a vivacious personality coupled with down-to-earth values. She can be unpredictable at times, but reliable when it comes to her grandkids.

Persona: Jewish Grandma

Fun Fact: Avrom Honig's 83-year-old grandmother, Bubbe, is the star of her popular, online kosher cooking show, *Feed Me Bubbe*. www.feedmebubbe.com

Bubbles

(pronounced bŭb-əls). 1. Something lacking substance. 2. A bundle of energy with money to spend on her latest boyfriend and of course, on her grandkids.

Persona: Popular Grandma

Bunya

(pronounced bŭn-yä). Do not be late when visiting Bunya, or you will be in big trouble.

Persona: Strict Ukrainian Grandma

Buster

(pronounced bŭst-ər). A rather big, husky woman who is not particularly fond of sitting and visiting.

Persona: Crabby Grandma

Grandma Story

One Irish-Catholic grandmother with an Italian last name from Boston was determined to be called Bubbe — a traditionally Jewish name for grandmother. Her family thought her idea was comical, but she prevailed, and "Bubbe Caputo" was born.

Cadillac (pronounced kä-dĭ-lək). 1. The best, magnificent. 2. Advice to son-in-laws: Do not mess up and call her "Old Battle-Axe!"

Persona: Maintenance-Free Grandma

CanCan (pronounced kăn-kăn). 1. Lively and risqué dance known for its high kicks. 2. Anything goes at this grandma's house.

Persona: Permissive Grandma

ChaChi (pronounced chă-chē). She is hard to keep up with! Whether power-walking with her friends or taking a yoga class, she is a woman on the go.

Persona: Former-Phys-Ed-Teacher Grandma

Cher (pronounced shĕr). 1. She is someone who is dear to her family and friends. 2. A superstar with a strong voice and outrageous costumes.

Persona: Flamboyant Grandma

Chickie (pronounced chĭk-ē). In a word: "hot-stuff!" Tight white jeans still look good on Chickie!

Persona: One-Good-Looking Grandma

Grandma Story

Growing up, she was affectionately called Chickie because of her golden hair and energetic personality. So, she declared that Chickie would be her Grandma name, too.

Cici

(pronounced sē-sē). Flirty and entertaining, Cici loves to throw a party. Hugs and kisses abound when you are with Cici!

Persona: Wet-Kisses Grandma

Cissy

(pronounced sĭs-ē). Can be a "sissy" when things do not go her way.

Persona: Grouchy Grandma

Coco

(pronounced kō-kō). Has great taste and impeccable clothes.

Persona: Sophisticated French Grandma

Fun Fact: Famous fashion designer Coco Chanel was born Gabrielle Chanel. Coco was her name during her brief career as a cabaret singer. She never married.

Contessa

(pronounced kŏn-tĕss-ä). Literally translated as an Italian Countess.

Persona: Eccentric-Self-Promoting Grandma

Fun Fact: Countess di Castiglione, better known as La Castiglione, was an Italian courtesan who achieved notoriety as a mistress of Emperor Napoleon III of France.

Coochee

(pronounced kōō-chē). When she tickles her grandchildren, she says, "Coochee-coo."

Persona: Silly Grandma

DaMa   (pronounced dä-mä). With her long leather coats and over-stuffed purses, you cannot miss DaMa.

Persona: American-Gangster Grandma

Dame   (pronounced dām). 1. A woman of rank and authority. 2. She is one grand broad.

Persona: Noble-and-Fiercely-Loyal Grandma

Fun Fact: The title of Dame is the female equivalent of Knighthood in the British honors system. In 1999, Queen Elizabeth II made Actress Elizabeth Taylor a Dame.

Dede   (pronounced dē-dē). Tall, thin and tan. She wears extra-large glasses with brightly colored frames and lenses.

Persona: Fashionista Grandma

Deli   (pronounced dĕl-ē). Deli is short for "Delicious."

Persona: Hot-and-Spicy Grandma

Ditti   (pronounced dĭt-tē). Super organized, she is ready to run any fundraising event or community program.

Persona: Give-Me-All-Your-Money Grandma

Fun Fact

Anna Jervis, the "Mother" of Mother's Day, remained unmarried and childless. Yet, she made sure all mothers were honored.

* * *

In 1914, President Woodrow Wilson made Mother's Day an official holiday.

Diva
(pronounced dē-vä). Diva never leaves home without an escort.

Persona: Hollywood-Socialite Grandma

Dodo
(pronounced dō-dō). She is not at her best first thing in the morning.

Persona: Need-My-Morning-Coffee Grandma

Doe
(pronounced dō). Her kind eyes adore her husband, Buck, and grandchildren.

Persona: Hiking-and-Camping Grandma

Dolly
(pronounced dŏl-ē). Think Hello Dolly. She is a woman with her nose in everyone's business trying to make the world a better place.

Persona: Life-is-a-Cabaret Grandma

Drama
(pronounced drä-mä). Whether she is on stage or off, there is always drama.

Persona: Broadway-Musical Grandma

Duchess
(pronounced dŭch-ĭs). Her exact age is completely unknown.

Persona: Royalty-Wanna-Be Grandma

Famous Grandma

Actress Joan Collins is Dodo

Egge
(pronounced ĕg-ē). She is not famous.

Persona: Plain Grandma

Eleanor
(pronounced əl-ē-nôr). Naturally big-busted. They now reside oh-so, very low.

Persona: Old-Fashioned Grandma

Fun Fact: Former First Lady Eleanor Roosevelt was known as "Grand-Mère."

Elisi
(pronounced əl-lē-sē). She still wears her chestnut-colored hair straight and to her waist.

Persona: American-Cherokee Grandma

Estee
(pronounced əs-të). Literally translated as "this grand-mother is a star."

Persona: Shining-Bright French Grandma

Evie
(pronounced ē-vē). She is a well-off woman who uses her advantages to provide for others.

Persona: Silver-Spoon Grandma

Celebrity Grandma Story:

Evelyn Lauder is the daughter-in-law of makeup empire co-founder Estee Lauder. Evelyn's grandchildren call her **Evie**.

Evie created the Breast Cancer Research Fund in 1993.

Fancy

(pronounced făn-sē). 1. Superior grade. 2. Her afternoon tea time ritual is a cup of Darjeeling and croissants.

Persona: Daily-Rituals-Are-Important Grandma

Fanny

(pronounced făn-nē). Fanny is one practical grandma. She still sports her circa 1985 fanny pack daily, so she is ready for any emergency.

Persona: Function-Over-Fashion Grandma

Fifi

(pronounced fē-fē). She is never short on advice.

Persona: Blabber-Mouth Grandma

Flemy

(pronounced flə-mē). Her one and only annoying habit is that she constantly clears her throat.

Persona: All-Stuffed-Up Grandma

Foxy

(pronounced fŏks-sē). 1. Cunningly shrewd; physically attractive. 2. Very comfortable in her own skin, but completely untrustworthy.

Persona: Foxy-Lady Grandma

Frannie

(pronounced fră-nē). Loves to tell tall tales and be the center of attention.

Persona: Stretching-the-Truth-Just-a-Bit Grandma

Fufoo

(pronounced fōō-fōō). She is not everyone's cup of tea.

Persona: High-and-Mighty Grandma

Fun Fact:
The month of September has the most births.
* * *
November has the least.

G   (**pronounced jē**). "G" is a late bloomer feminist who likes to attend rallies, marches and protests.

Persona: Feminist Grandma

Gabby   (**pronounced gǎ-bē**). Inclined to talk too much.

Persona: Chatty Grandma

Gada   (**pronounced gä-dä**). Likes to have structured, calm time with her grandkids. That means no amusement or water park trips with Gada.

Persona: Stiff-as-a-Board Grandma

Gaga   (**pronounced gä-gä**). 1. Crazy, foolish. 2. Not afraid to wield her cane at any adult or small child.

Persona: Aggressive Grandma

Gaia   (**pronounced jē-ä**). Greek goddess of the earth.

Persona: Mother-Nature Greek Grandma

Galini   (**pronounced gǎ-lē-nē**). Galini is all about living life with flair and roaming to far-off places of the world. Her husbands can rarely keep up with her.

Persona: Worldly Grandma

Gam   (**pronounced gǎm**). Long-time soap opera devotee.

Persona: Day-Time-TV Grandma

Grandma Story:

One grandmother-to-be joked she was actually
"G.G. = God's Girlfriend"

Gamcha   (pronounced găm-chă). Some days she just cannot be found.

Persona: Wandering Grandma

Gamma   (pronounced găm-ma). Her stern looks convey all.

Persona: Woman-of-Few-Words Grandma

Gammlemor   (pronounced găm-lĕ-mōr). Sophisticated and well-heeled, she expects good behavior at all times. Pressed pantsuits are a favorite of Gammlemor.

Persona: Well-Bred Norwegian Grandma

Gamommie   (pronounced găm-mŏm-ē). On the weekends, Gamommie can be found running local 5K road races.

Persona: Exercise-Fanatic Grandma

Gammy   (pronounced găm-mē). 1. Showing resolute spirit: plucky. 2. Her single strand of pearls and matching earrings belie her wild past.

Persona: American-Political-Family Grandma

Gammy-Goose   (pronounced găm-mē-gōōs). White-haired and wild. Goose comes and goes as she pleases.

Persona: As-the-Wind-Blows Grandma

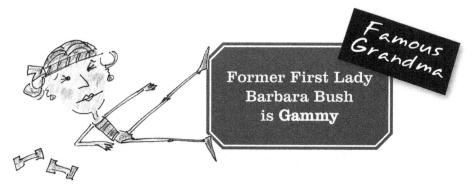

Famous Grandma

Former First Lady
Barbara Bush
is **Gammy**

Gams (pronounced găms). Gams has great legs.

Persona: Rockette Grandma

Gayga (pronounced gā-gă). Her direct involvement with her grandchildren is sending timely birthday presents.

Persona: Stand-off-ish Grandma

Gee (pronounced jē). A happy name for a happy person.

Persona: Cheerful Grandma

Gigi (pronounced jē-jē). Gigi never forgets to put on her makeup, or at least lipstick, before leaving the house.

Persona: Everybody-loves Grandma

Gigia (pronounced j-jē-ä). Gigia is mysterious and very in-dependent.

Persona: Glorious Greek Grandma

Ginny (pronounced jĭn-nē). A down-to-earth woman made from scratch.

Persona: Worked-my-way-up-the-hard-way Grandma

Celebrity Grandma Story:

In March of 2011, Chef Paula Dean was a guest on *The Today Show* with Kathie Lee and Hoda Kotb. Hoda asked Paula, "What does your grandson call you?" Paula replied, "Well, there was a lot of arguing about that. My son suggested, "Big Mama." I told him if he called me Big Mama, I was going to kick his Big Ass right out of my will!"

Chef Paula Deen is **Ginny**.

Glamma

(pronounced glăm-mä). Glamma is glamorous and stylish. She looks younger than her years.

Persona: Hollywood Grandma

Fun Fact: Actress, Goldie Hawn is Glamma. Socialite, Ivana Trump is Glamma.

G-Ma

(pronounced jē-mä). A contemporary version of Grandma, G-Ma is confident and street smart. There is no "pulling the wool" over G-Ma's eyes!

Persona: Street-Smart Grandma

G-Mama

(pronounced jē-mä-mä). Is adamant about using the salutation *Ms.* not *Mrs.* She has been a feminist since the 70s.

Persona: Socially-Progressive Grandma

G-Mom

(pronounced jē-mŏm). Loves to crochet while watching those evening reality shows.

Persona: Evening-Couch-Potato Grandma

Goddess

(pronounced gŏd-ĭs). A woman of exceptional beauty and charm. She believes that being a woman is cool... you've got all this power.

Persona: I-Am-Woman-Hear-Me-Roar Grandma

Celebrity Grandma Story:
In the March 7, 2011 issue of *People* Magazine, Ivana Trump stated, "Calling me Grandma is out of the question. It is GLAM-MA!"

Go-Go (pronounced gō-gō). Just watch her go-go-go!

Persona: Multi-Tasking Grandma

Golda (pronounced gŏl-dä). Strong-willed, straight-talking, grey-bunned grandma.

Persona: Visionary Grandma

Fun Fact: Golda Meir is considered to be the "Grandmother of the Jewish people."

Golly (pronounced gŏl-ē). She is someone who does not take herself too seriously.

Persona: Joyful Grandma

Gommy (pronounced gŏm-mē). She is all the best of Mommy!

Persona: Superlative Grandma

Goose (pronounced gōōs). Fluffy pancakes with powdered sugar are her signature breakfast.

Persona: Early-Bird-Gets-the-Worm Grandma

Gra (pronounced grä). She can be tough and firm, but her grandchildren make her all soft and cuddly.

Persona: Old-Softy Grandma

Grady

(pronounced grā-dē). A party Grandmother! It quickly becomes "5:00 PM somewhere" when you are with her.

Persona: Happy-Hour Grandma

Gram

(pronounced grăm). Gram's candy drawer is just at the right height filled with every kind of forbidden, sweet treat!

Persona: All-American Grandma

Grama

(pronounced grăm-mə). Her favorite book is *Heloise Household Hints*.

Persona: Neat-and-Tidy Grandma

Gramarama

(pronounced grăm-ă-rămă). She has a great laugh—her whole body shakes when she laughs.

Persona: Giggling Grandma

Grammy

(pronounced grăm-mē). Napping on Grammy's needle-point pillows will certainly leave an impression.

Persona: American-Sampler Grandma

Gramsy

(pronounced grăm-sē). Whimsical chicken parapher-nalia decorate her home.

Persona: Quirky Grandma

Create your own unique name!
Create your own grandma name by merg-
ing "Gran" with your name.

Gran + Nancy = Grancy
Gran + Angela = Granela

Grand   (pronounced grănd). She may not be large, but she sure is in-charge!

Persona: Gives-the-Orders Grandma

Fun Fact: Actress Julie Andrews is Grand Julie; Jackie Kennedy Onassis was Grand Jackie.

Grand Dame   (pronounced grănd-dām). No other qualities are more important to her than lineage and pedigree.

Persona: Snobby Grandma

Grand DiggityDog   (pronounced grănd-dĭg-ĭtē-dôg). Stray animals know just where to go!

Persona: Animal-Lover Grandma

Grandma   (pronounced grănd´mă). Affectionate and kind. She cannot resist tickling and squeezing her grandkids when she sees them.

Persona: The-Best-Kind-Of Grandma

Grandma Great   (pronounced grănd-mă-grāt). Oriental rugs and large oil paintings accent her large Victorian home.

Persona: Victorian-Era Grandma

Famous Grandmas

Former Supreme Court Justice
Sandra Day O'Connor is **Grandma**.

✳ ✳ ✳

Former First Lady Jackie Kennedy was
Grand Jackie.

Grandmama (pronounced grănd-mă-mä). She refers often to her life in the old country.

Persona: Nostalgic Grandma

Fun Fact: Grandmama was the grandmother in the 1960s TV show, *The Addams Family*. Aka, Granny Frump.

Grandmamy (pronounced grănd-mă-mee). Has taken care of so many children she has lost count.

Persona: Surrogate-Mom Grandma

Grandmaw (pronounced grănd-mô). Even with her thick southern drawl, her words are never mistaken by anyone.

Persona: Confederate Grandma

Grand-Mère (pronounced grănd-měr). Never goes anywhere without her tiny, well-groomed Chihuahua.

Persona: City-of-Love French Grandma

Grandmissy (pronounced grănd-mis-ē). Voted most popular girl in high school.

Persona: Prom-Queen Grandma

Grandmom (pronounced grănd-mŏm). Her "Don't mess with Grandma" bumper sticker says it all.

Persona: Military Grandma

Famous Grandma

Former First Lady Eleanor Roosevelt was **Grand-Mère**.

Grandmuck   (pronounced grănd-muk).   Lives on a backroad, swampy property.

Persona: Sporadic-Electricity Grandma

Grandnan   (pronounced grănd-nan). She never scolds, just wrings her hands on her apron.

Persona: Old-Fashioned Grandma

Grandnana   (pronounced grănd-nă-nə). She still likes to ride her horses first thing in the morning.

Persona: Old-Money Grandma

GranGram   (pronounced grăn-grăm). Everyone is so proud that Gran-Gram wins the prized pie contest every year at the local fair!

Persona: Loves-to-Bake Grandma

GranGran   (pronounced grăn-grăn). She never flinches when filleting fish freshly caught by her grandkids.

Persona: Cape-Cod Grandma

Granma   (pronounced grăn-mă). Never lets little ones go outside or go to bed with wet hair.

Persona: Old-Wives-Tales Grandma

FUN FACT:

"Granny Clampett" was the redneck grandmother on the 1960s hit TV show, *The Beverly Hillbillies*.

Granmomma (pronounced grăn-mŏm-mä). Granmomma was the first of her girlfriends to earn an athletic varsity letter jacket in high school.

Persona: Sporty Grandma

Granno (pronounced grăn-no). Enjoys all of her grandchildren's performances.

Persona: My-Grandchild-is #1 Grandma

Granny (pronounced grăn-nē). An authentic, veritable delight. On any given day, you might find Granny sitting on her porch swing with a shotgun in her hands.

Persona: Grits-and-Gravy Grandma

Grannyma (pronounced grăn-nē-mă). Grannyma's worn-out blue jean overalls are relics, but they look perfect on her.

Persona: Southern Grandma

Grannymama (pronounced grăn-nē-mă-mä). No one can handle a John Deere tractor like Grannymama.

Persona: Down-on-the-Farm Grandma

Granzilla (pronounced grăn-zil-ä). Typically reserved for mothers-in-law; monster grandmother.

Persona: Scary Grandma

Famous Grandma

President Franklin Delano Roosevelt's mother, Sara Delano Roosevelt, was known as **Granny.**

Gree-Gree (pronounced grē-grē). Gree-Gree lives high up on a hill, making frequent family visitors infrequent. She likes it that way.

Persona: Solitary Grandma

Gremmon (pronounced grə-mŏn). Fancy hats and ladies luncheons at the club are her pastime favorites.

Persona: Protestant Grandma

Grossmutter (pronounced grōs-mut-ər). Neat, tidy and never "colors outside the lines" is Grossmutter.

Persona: Stern German Grandma

Gumma (pronounced gum-mä). Gummas have a firm, neurotic center. There is no telling in what sort of mood she will be.

Persona: Psycho Grandma

Guppy (pronounced gup-ē). Clicks her car lock button many times to make sure that it is definitely locked and secured.

Persona: Paranoid Grandma

Famous Clown Grandma

The famous "Grandma Clown" in the Big Apple Circus is no ma, technically.

Grandma Clown is Barry Lubin, who says he can play the role, because he knew both his grandmothers very well.

Happy

(pronounced hăp-ē). She likes to say, "A heart that loves is always young."

Persona: Old-Greek-Saying Grandma

Hillary

(pronounced hĭl-er-ē). She enjoys debating about international issues.

Persona: Political Grandma

Hippy

(pronounced hĭp-ē). Hippy is very cool and likes wearing long, flowing skirts and hemp necklaces.

Persona: American-1960s Grandma

Hon

(pronounced hŭn). Fall is her favorite time of year because she can take her grandchildren apple picking and then bake apple pies.

Persona: Seasonal Grandma

Honey

(pronounced hŭn-ē). Honey is as sweet as her name. She remembers those long-forgotten Sunday drives.

Persona: American-Nostalgia Grandma

Fun Fact: Honey Bees are one of the social bees that produce honey.

Huggie

(pronounced hŭg-ē). She is tough, dry and dependable.

Persona: Waterproof Grandma

Hussy

(pronounced hŭs-ē). Hussy is slightly immoral, very brazen and just a bit mischievous.

Persona: Oh-No-Here-She-Comes Grandma

Jadda   (pronounced jā-dä). She likes to say, "Every age has its book."

Persona: Old-Arabic-Saying Grandma

Jammie   (pronounced jăm-ē). You never get too old for a sleepover at Jammie's.

Persona: Flannel-Nightgown Grandma

Jazzy   (pronounced jăzz-ē). She loves listening to her jazz radio station.

Persona: Dancing-in-the-Kitchen Grandma

JinJin   (pronounced jĭn-jĭn). A self-proclaimed artist. She enjoys drawing and painting with her grandchildren.

Persona: Artistic Grandma

Jiggy   (pronounced jĭg-ē). Look out for flying arms and legs when Jiggy hits the dance floor with her grandkids.

Persona: Two-Left-Feet Grandma

JoJo   (pronounced jō-jō). Animated, acute and utterly self-possessed.

Persona: Self-Absorbed Grandma

Famous Grandma

The famous 1930s–1950s film actress, Joan Crawford, was known as **JoJo**.

JuJu (pronounced jū-jū). She has supernatural powers.

Persona: West-African Grandma

June (pronounced jūn). June likes to sleep in on most days.

Persona: Summer-Vacation Grandma

Juno (pronounced jūn-ō). Juno was the Queen of the Gods.

Persona: Roman-goddess Grandma

Fun Fact: Her symbol is the peacock. Juno's husband is Jupiter, king of the gods.

Kitty (pronounced kit-tē). Husband #4 thinks she is beautiful.

Persona: Matrimonial Grandma

Kryptonite (pronounced krip-tō-nīt). She has been working out faithfully with her sexy, young personal trainer.

Persona: Long-Time-YMCA-Member Grandma

Kupuna Wahine (pronounced kä-pōō-nə-wä-hē-nə). A former, Hawaiian Airlines stewardess who placed leis on de-planing passengers.

Persona: Beautiful Hawaiian Grandma

Famous Queen Grandmas

Princes William and Harry call their Grandma, Queen Elizabeth II, Granny. The Princes called their Great-Grandma, Queen Elizabeth I, Lizzy.

Lady
(pronounced lā-dē). She is a well-mannered woman with high standards. An imported, one-of-a-kind, chic handbag can always be found dangling from her arm.

Persona: American-Royalty Grandma

Lala
(pronounced lä-lä). She still sneaks that daily cigarette.

Persona: Where-Did-She-Go-Now Grandma

Lalo
(pronounced lä-lō). She radiates positive energy.

Persona: Laughter-Is-the-Best-Medicine Grandma

Lela
(pronounced lā-lä). She has never veered from her morning ritual: full body stretch, ten toe touches, brush hair, moisturize and then make strong coffee.

Persona: Ritualistic Spanish Grandma

LiLi
(pronounced lē-lē). LiLi usually has something up her sleeve. It is an unpredictable adventure with Lili.

Persona: Dependable-but-Unpredictable Grandma

Lily
(pronounced lĭl-ē). Headbands keep her hair neat and tidy.

Persona: Pure-and-Refined Grandma

Fun Fact: The lily flower symbolizes purity and beauty

FAMOUS GRANDMA:
Actress Blythe Danner
(Gwyneth Paltrow's Mom)
is **Lalo**.

Lola   (pronounced lō-lä). The name Lola conjures up sultry images and colorful clothes. Weekly Senior salsa dancing keeps her in shape.

Persona: Disco Spanish Grandma

Lolly   (pronounced lŏl-ē). With her crisp, white tennis outfit and hair perfectly twisted into a bun, she can always be spotted on the court.

Persona: Upper-Class Grandma

Love   (pronounced lŭv). Watch out for those great, big, red lipstick kisses.

Persona: Glamour-Pus Grandma

Lovey   (pronounced lŭv-ē). Hates to miss out on any event during the social season. She is more comfortable socializing with those on the social register.

Persona: Socially-Prominent Grandma

Fun Fact: Mrs. Lovey Howell was the rich, spoiled socialite on 1960s comedy TV show, *Gilligan's Island*.

Lucky   (pronounced lŭk-ē). "Diligence is the mother of good luck." ~ words of Benjamin Franklin.

Persona: Find-a-Penny-Pick-it-Up Grandma

Lulu   (pronounced lōō-lōō). Believes her grandchildren are angels on earth.

Persona: Heavenly Grandma

Ma (pronounced mä). Usually can be found meddling in someone's affairs.

Persona: Way-Too-Involved Grandma

Madonna (pronounced mä-don-nä). Like a virgin?

Persona: Holy-Roller Grandma

Mae (pronounced mā). A life-long librarian who would not think of reading anything but classic literature to her grandkids.

Persona: Literary Grandma

Maga (pronounced mä-gä). Habit of purchasing unnecessary tchotchkes for her grandchildren and daughters-in-law.

Persona: Saturday-Yard-Sales Grandma

Majesty (pronounced mə-jes-tē). 1. State of being impressive or dignified. 2. She is vain and unapproachable.

Persona: Nose-in-the-Air Grandma

Maia (pronounced mī-ə). Literally translated as Good Mother.

Persona: Good Greek Grandma

Mama (pronounced mä-mä). She has the magic of maternal family leadership (or is it dictatorship?).

Persona: Controlling Grandma

Celebrity Grandma:

Actor Mathew McConaghey's mother is MaMac.

Mamma-Joon (pronounced mă-mă-joon). Literally translated as mama dear.

Persona: Farsi Grandma

Mamie (pronounced mä-mē). Still prefers girdles.

Persona: Old-Fashioned-Contraption Grandma

MaMoo (pronounced mä-mōō). MaMoo regularly trolls Marshalls for bargains. Hard-to-find household items and trinkets are her specialty. A bargain is a bargain!

Persona: American-Spender Grandma

Manamma (pronounced mă-nă-mă). Manama is like a Mexican jumping bean—she just can't sit still.

Persona: Jumpy Mexican Grandma

Manita (pronounced măn-ē-tă). Spanish term of endearment for Mother. A hot bowl of Manita's homemade soup can make everything all right.

Persona: Special Spanish Grandma

Manny (pronounced măn-ē). Menswear is what she wears.

Persona: She-Wears-the-Pants Grandma

Marme (pronounced mär-mē). Think Little Women. She is someone with kind words and heartfelt empathy for everyone she meets.

Persona: Old-Fashioned-Hard-Working Grandma

Martha (pronounced mär-thă). One 99-year-old great-grandmother felt that she clearly was not old enough to be called Grandma, so they called her Martha.

Persona: Don't-Mess-With Grandma

Maw-Maw   (pronounced mô-mô). Would not be caught without her flesh colored pantyhose.

Persona: Good-Southern-Manners Grandma

May   (pronounced mā). Has been dutifully serving for years on the local Women's and Garden Club boards.

Persona: American-Civic-Duty Grandma

MeMa   (pronounced mē-mä). Be cautious when approaching MeMa about the family history. Some parts of family history are "not to be discussed."

Persona: This-Doesn't-Leave-The-Table Grandma

MeMaw   (pronounced mē-mô). She is not one to back down from a fight, but diplomatic in her discussions. You can always count on MeeMaw to "have your back."

Persona: Old-Faithful-and-Dependable Grandma

Famous Grandma

Country Singer Naomi Judd is **MeMaw**

"A house needs a Grandmother in it."

—Louisa May Alcott, Author

MeMo

(pronounced mē-mō). Can be a worrier, but will put on a happy face to disguise her feelings.

Persona: Ulcer Grandma

MeMom

(pronounced mē-mŏm). Unflappable and dependable. She is a Grandma who you can confide in without judgment.

Persona: Mum's-the-Word Grandma

Mica

(pronounced mī-kä). Rules and order, clearly defined by Mica, must be adhered to upon entering her home.

Persona: My-Way-or-the-Highway Serbian Grandma

Mim

(pronounced mĭm). Super sophisticated with flawless taste. She enjoys frequenting local art galleries, theatres and museums with her grandkids.

Persona: PhD Grandma

Mimi

(pronounced mĭm-ē or mē-mē). She is one smart, savvy grandmother. She emails, texts and even tweets with her grandchildren!

Persona: Tech-Savvy-Totally-With-It Grandma

> "Painting's not important. The important thing is that we keep busy."
>
> —Grandma Moses
> American Folk Artist, 1860-1961

Mimmé   (pronounced mĭm-mā). From Portuguese descent, she is a woman who works hard at all that she does, but sets special time aside for family. She avails herself to everyone, but also takes care of herself.

Persona: Dedicated Portuguese Grandma

Moma   (pronounced mŏm-mə). Her car proudly displays bumper stickers from every grandchild's college!

Persona: College-Fund Grandma

Momanana   (pronounced mŏm-ä-nă-nä). It is an anagram, "A Nana Mom."

Persona: Scrabble-Playing Grandma

Momma   (pronounced mŏm-mä). A career woman who relies on her crock pot every day.

Persona: Working-Girl Grandma

Momme   (pronounced mŏm-may). Even when the wind blows, Momme's hair stays in place!

Persona: Hair-Spray Grandma

Mom-Mom   (pronounced mŏm-mŏm). She is twice the fun!

Persona: Double-Trouble Grandma

Famous Grandma

Vice President Joe Biden's Mom is Mom-Mom.

MoMo

(pronounced mō-mō). She is a former piano teacher who loves playing classical music for her grandchildren.

Persona: Musical Grandma

Moo

(pronounced mōō). Moo carries crackling, plastic-wrapped candy in her jacket pockets.

Persona: Sweet-Tooth Grandma

MopMop

(pronounced mŏp-mŏp). Speaks up regularly at the monthly town hall meetings.

Persona: Mayor Grandma

MoreNana

(pronounced môr-na-nä). What grandchild would not want more of Nana?

Persona: American Nana

MorMor

(pronounced môr-môr). Literally, "Mother's Mother."

Persona: Swedish Grandma

MoxieMom

(pronounced mŏks-ē-mŏm). She has a unique, although somewhat bitter, flavor to her.

Persona: She-Can-Hit-a-Nerve Grandma

FUN FACT:
National Grandparents Day
is celebrated the first Sunday after
Labor Day annually!

Mum　(pronounced mŭm). You will always find Mum dressed properly with matching shoes, pocketbook and hat.

Persona: British Grandma

Mummi　(pronounced mōō-mē). She likes to say, "A bird in the hand is worth ten in the bush."

Persona: Old-Finnish-Saying Grandma

Mummica　(pronounced mŭm-mī-kā). Meat and potatoes are staple dishes of Mummica. They just come in different dinner combinations every time.

Persona: 1950s Grandma

Mummy　(pronounced mŭm-ē). She would wear spandex under her bathing suit if she could.

Persona: All-Wrapped-Up Grandma

Mutti　(pronounced mōō-tē). She likes to say, "Too many cooks spoil the broth."

Persona: Old-German-Saying Grandma

Fun Fact:

The National Cowgirl Museum, located in Fort Worth, TX, is dedicated to honoring women who have distinguished themselves by exemplifying the pioneer spirit of the American West.

Sandra Day O'Connor, First Woman Supreme Court Justice: Hall of Fame Member (Inducted 2002)

Nai Nai   (pronounced nī-nī). She likes to say, "One generation plants the trees; another gets the shade."

Persona: Old-Chinese-Saying Grandma

Namma   (pronounced năm-mă). Loves her Florida home in the winter and her upstate New York home in the summer.

Persona: Snow-Bird Grandma

Nan   (pronounced năn). A hipper, more contemporary Nana. She still colors her hair every month.

Persona: Weekly-Beauty-Salon Grandma

Nana   (pronounced nă-nä). Loving, kind and generous describes Nana. She has a passion for cleaning her house and ironing everyone's clothes.

Persona: Loves-You-Unconditionally Grandma

Nana-Grandma (pronounced nă-nä-gr̆and-mă). She never says "No" to any grandchild's request.

Persona: Sweetheart Grandma

Nanny   (pronounced nă-nē). Her beach house is located near the best clam shack ever!

Persona: Down-by-the-Bay Grandma

Create your own contemporary name!

Create a new Grandma name by making a diminutive of your own name:

Lisa = Lili
Denise = Dede
Susan = SuSu

Nanoo
(pronounced năn-nōō). Sturdy and well-built. A wool sweater is all she needs in sub-zero weather.

Persona: Thick-Skinned Grandma

Fun Fact: "Nanoo Nanoo" was the salutation used by TV character Mork on the series "Mork and Mindy." Robin Williams played Mork and Pam Dawson played Mindy.

Nauna
(pronounced nôn-nä). Dusting is her specialty—whether at her home or yours!

Persona: Got-to-Keep-Moving Italian Grandma

Nem
(pronounced něm). Little girls love playing at Nem's makeup vanity overflowing with the latest makeup products and even false eyelashes!

Persona: Makeup Grandma

Nini
(pronounced nē-nē). Doting, loving and somewhat scatter-brained.

Persona: Dizzy Grandma

Fun Fact: When texting, NiNi is short for saying Night-Night or Good-Night.

NinnaNana
(pronounced nǐn-ä-nä-nä). She likes to say, "Old wine and friends improve with age."

Persona: Old-Italian-Saying Grandma

Famous Grandma

Comedian Joan Rivers is Nana-New-Face.

Nonna   (pronounced nŏn-nă). Authentic Nonnas call their homemade, tomato sauce "gravy."

Persona: Eat-Some-then-Eat-Some-More Italian Grandma

Fun Fact: Giada DeLaurentiss, famous Food Network Chef, called her grandma, Nonna Luna because she was the first one to show Giada the moon.

Nonnie   (pronounced nŏn-nē). Not as old-fashioned as Nonna, but appreciates big family dinners. Cooking is her favorite pastime.

Persona: Always-Cooking Italian Grandma

Nonnina   (pronounced nŏn-nină). A petite version of traditional Nonna. When excited, she speaks in both Italian and English.

Persona: Tiny-but-Tough Italian Grandma

Nooney   (pronounced noon-nē). A very self-sufficient grandma who drives herself everywhere.

Persona: Super-Independent Grandma

NunNun   (pronounced nun-nun). Like a 1950s Catholic nun, she can be somewhat rigid and demanding.

Persona: Leader-of-the-Pack Grandma

Fun Fact: Mother Theresa of Calcutta was a famous nun.

Famous Grandma

Actress Pricilla Presley is **Nonna.**

Obaachan (pronounced ō-bä-chan). She takes very small, but very quick steps.

Persona: Light-on-her-Feet Japanese Grandma

Obaasan (pronounced ō-bä-san). Although she rarely smiles, she cares deeply for her family.

Persona: Quiet Japanese Grandma

Oldemor (pronounced ōl-de-môr). Literally translates as Great Grandma.

Persona: Norwegian Great-Grandma

Ona Great (pronounced ōna-grāt). One whose grace is amazing.

Persona: Princess Grandma

Oopsy (pronounced ōp-sē). She is strangely clumsy.

Persona: Head-in-the-Clouds Grandma

Oma (pronounced ō-mə). Always ready to take off with grandkids. She is extremely proud of her heritage.

Persona: On-the-Move German Grandma

Ouma (pronounced ōō-mä). She likes to say, "It is better to trust the eyes rather than the ears."

Persona: Old-German-Saying Grandma

Famous Grandma

Actor Leonardo DeCaprio's Grandma is Oma.

Petunia (pronounced pə-tōōn-yä). 1. Wide funnel-shaped spring flower. 2. Every Sunday in spring, Petunia heads to church wearing her fashionable Easter hat, fancy dress and white gloves.

Persona: Spring-into-Action Grandma

Phar-Mor (pronounced fär-môr). With her graying blonde hair knotted perfectly in a bun, Phar-Mor looks ready to undertake any job with efficiency and beauty.

Persona: Pretty Swedish Grandma

Picky (pronounced pĭk-ē). 1. Literally translated as fussy. 2. When ordering at restaurants, she asks so many questions that it is embarrassing.

Persona: Can't-Make-up-Her-Mind Grandma

Plucky (pronounced plŭk-ē). She is notably spirited and courageous.

Persona: Gutsy Grandma

PoPo (pronounced pō-pō). She likes to say, "Walls have ears and little pots, too."

Persona: Old-Chinese-Saying Grandma

Pretty (pronounced prĭt-ē). Loves wearing her 100% virgin-wool navy-blue pea-coat with shiny brass buttons.

Persona: Never-Goes-out-of-Style Grandma

Principessa (pronounced prĭn-sĕ-pĕs-ä). She still has that great sparkle in her clear baby-blue eyes.

Persona: Can-Light-up-the-Room Italian Grandma

Quacky

(pronounced kwăk-ē). Never leaves her house without "putting on" her eyelashes and eyebrows.

Persona: Vanity Grandma

Queenie

(pronounced kwēn-nē). Pedicures and manicures are a favorite weekly indulgence of Queenie.

Persona: High-Maintenance Grandma

Quirky

(pronounced kwurk-ē). She does not seek the limelight.

Persona: Do-Your-Own-Thing Grandma

Regal

(pronounced rē-gəl). Regal's skirts are hemmed precisely two inches below her kneecap.

Persona: Up-Tight Grandma

Renegade

(pronounced rĕn-ĭ-gād). Homeownership never interested Renegade…she prefers to rent so she can roam freely.

Persona: Free-Spirit Grandma

Robo

(pronounced rō-bō). She is just going through the motions at this stage.

Persona: It-is-What-it-Is Grandma

Ruler

(pronounced rōō-lər). Strict and proper.

Persona: No-Fun Grandma

Rusty

(pronounced rŭs-tē). Years of hoarding now limits the number of family members who can visit her.

Persona: Gotta-Have-It Grandma

Sassy

(pronounced săs-sē). A take-charge grandma who is always full of ideas and adventure. World traveling and safaris are her specialty!

Persona: Adventurous Grandma

Scooby

(pronounced skōō-bē). Her 1979 Chevy Impala convertible still passes inspection every year.

Persona: Car-Aficionado Grandma

Sean-mhathair

(pronounced shan-waw-her). She likes to say, "A face without freckles is like a sky without stars."

Persona: Old-Irish-Saying Grandma

Snazzy

(pronounced snaz-ē). 1. Attractive in a flashy or showy way. 2. She believes that dressing in animal print clothes will diffuse a hot flash.

Persona: Flashily-Attractive Grandma

Snookie

(pronounced snŏŏk-ē). She is someone who rarely sleeps. You never know when Snookie might show up.

Persona: Never-Ceases-to-Amaze Grandma

Sugar

(pronounced shŏŏ-gər). Relatives and strangers are always welcome drop-ins at Sugars. She likes to say, "Any friend of yours is a friend of mine."

Persona: Sweet-and-Friendly Grandma

Sunny

(pronounced sun-nee). She is bright and cheerful.

Persona: You-Are-My-Sunshine Grandma

Tata (pronounced **ta-ta**). She is engaging and dismissive at the same time.

Persona: Gets-Things-Moving Grandma

Fun Fact: Philanthropist Charlotte Ford, daughter of Henry Ford II, is called Tata.

Tita (pronounced **tē-ta**). She likes to say, "An ounce of mother is worth a pound of clergy."

Persona: Old-Spanish-Saying Grandma

Tootsie (pronounced **tŭt-sē**). Tootsie looks forward to her Friday night bar-hopping with co-workers.

Persona: Never-Grew-Up Grandma

Tricksie (pronounced **trik-sē**). Tricksie can be somewhat eccentric because she is older and she does not care what people think of her.

Persona: Drinks-Right-out-of-the-Bottle Grandma

Tutu (pronounced **tōō-tōō**). She is a humble, plain-spoken woman willing to sacrifice for her grandchildren. Nickname is Toot.

Persona: Hawaiian Grandma

Tutu Wahine (pronounced **tōō-tōō-wä-hēn-e**). She is peaceful.

Persona: Hawaiian Grandma

Famous Grandma

President Obama's Grandma was Toot.

Umma

(pronounced ōō-mä). Umma's mixed heritage makes her unique and mysterious.

Persona: One-Very-Interesting Grandma

Ummy

(pronounced ōō-mē). She prefers to stretch her elastic waist pants comfortably over her tummy.

Persona: Unfashionable Grandma

Va

(pronounced vä). She likes to say, "Stumbling is not falling."

Persona: Old-Portuguese-Saying Grandma

Vela

(pronounced vā-lă). Vela is a dreamer who has big plans for her grandchildren.

Persona: Wishful-Thinking Latin Grandma

Fun Fact: Vela is a constellation known as "the Sail."

Vieja

(pronounced vē-ä-hä). The literal translation is "old," but this Vieja brings life to everyone around her!

Persona: Vivacious Spanish Grandma

Voltage

(pronounced vol-taj). Her sharp tongue and quick wit will keep you on your toes.

Persona: Live-Wire Grandma

Vovo

(pronounced vō-vō). A strong woman who is not afraid of hard work or of intimidating people. Her slightly larger hands are indicative of her hard working Portuguese ancestors.

Persona: Strongest Portuguese Grandma

Walita

(pronounced wôl-ē-tä). When highly agitated she reverts back to speaking Spanish (loudly and quickly!).

Persona: Don't-Get-Me-Started Mexican Grandma

WaWa

(pronounced wä-wä). Super spunky!

Persona: Endless-Energy Grandma

Wella

(pronounced wel-ä). Wella tries to be "politically correct." She reluctantly traded her mink coat for a faux fur.

Persona: Trying-to-be-a-Responsible-Citizen Grandma

Whirly

(pronounced wurl-ē). It is short for "Whirlwind."

Persona: Cyclone Grandma

Wippe

(pronounced wip-ē). Wippe never has a bad word to say about anyone.

Persona: Sees-Only-the-Good Grandma

Xena

(pronounced zēn-yə). Every Halloween, she excitedly puts on her brown leather Xena, the Princess Warrior costume.

Persona: Fantasy Grandma

YaYa

(pronounced yä-yä). Her bumper sticker says, "Sexy Greek Senior Citizen."

Persona: High-Life Grandma

Yia-Yia (pronounced yä-yä). Like the ancient Greek plays of long ago, Yia-Yia can be obscure and controversial.

Persona: Not-Sure-What-She-Is-Thinking Greek Grandma

Yogie (pronounced yōg-ee). Currently seeking peace and serenity in her grandmother phase of life.

Persona: Zen Grandma

Yoo-Hoo (pronounced yōō-hōō). She is the dreaded busy-body, nosy neighbor who will greet you with a big "Yoo-Hoo!"

Persona: You-Can-Hear-Her-a-Mile-Away Grandma

Zannie (pronounced zān-nē). Willing to try new, radical youth potions to ward off aging.

Persona: Celebrity Grandma

Zippy (pronounced zip-ē). Quick and agile. In the backyard, she will still attempt a cartwheel for her grandkids.

Persona: BENGAY Grandma

ZuZu (pronounced zōō-zōō). She is adorable with her tight, curly, white, cottonball-shaped hairdo.

Persona: Just-a-Very-Nice Grandma

Famous Grandma

Actress Suzanne Summers is Zannie.

> "When nothing is going well, call your Grandmother."

> —Old Italian Proverb

PART III

Grandmother
Stories

Grandma Name Stories

Zeni

One clever grandmother reversed her middle name. Her full name is Sarah Inez Crawford Lee, and her new grandmother name is "Zeni."

Lolly-Pop

One witty grandma decided since grandpa was going to be "Pop," she would be "Lolly" making them "Lolly-Pop."

Lulu

Grandma's name was Lucy, but her husband of 48 years always called her Lulu and so did her grandchildren. Then, Lulu decided to rename her husband from "Grandpa" to "Papa" because she thought "Lulu & Papa" sounded better together!

Martha

One 99-year-old great-grandmother felt that she clearly was not old enough to be called Grandma, so they call her "Martha."

Sassy

One grandma, who owns a house on the Connecticut shore, loves sailing with her grandkids and world traveling. She declared that her rightful, perfectly apt grandma name would be "Sassy." So, Sassy it is.

Amazing Grandmas

Oldest Mom Grandma

The world's oldest Mom is Omkari Panwar. She was 72 when she gave birth to twins in India in 2008. The world's second oldest Mom is Rosanna Dalla Corte. She was 63 when she gave birth in Italy in 1994.

Athletic Grandma

Sue Oldham, a 64-year-old Perth grandmother, became the oldest woman to swim the English Channel on August 9, 2010. She completed the crossing in 17 hours and 31 minutes.

Queen of Rock 'n Roll Grandma

Tina Turner, a 71-year-old grandma and great-grandma, can still rock a skin-tight outfit wearing spiked heels at her sold-out concerts!

Internet Grandma

Maria Amelia Lopez, a Spanish grandmother, became an Internet sensation after dubbing herself the "world's oldest blogger." Lopez later wrote, "On December 23rd 2006, my grandson gave me a present, this blog, when I was 95 years old...and my life changed...now, I can communicate and interact with the world."

PART IV

International Grandmother Names

Names by Country/Language

African
Ouma
Makhulu
Ogog (Zulu)

Bosnian
Baba
Deda Nena

Chinese
Nai Nai
Po Po
Wai po
Zu mu

Czech
Babicka
Babinka Babi

Danish
Bedstemor
Bomma
Farmor
Mormor

Dutch
Grootmoeder
Oma
Omi

Eskimo
Aanak
Annatsiaq

Fijian
Bubu Yalewa
Mbu mbu

Finnish
Isoaiti
Mummi
Mummo

Flemish
Bomma
Bonbonneki
Bonnie My
Mamy

French
Grand Maman
Grandmere
Memere
Mimi

German
Grossmutter
Oma
Omi

Greek
Gigia
Yaya
YiaYia

Hawaiian
Toot
Tutu
Tutu Wahine

Hebrew
Savta
Safta

Hindi
Daa-de-ma

Indian
Ajja
Daaii
Dida
Yhakur-ma

Indonesian
Nenek
Mbah putri
Eyang putri
Eni
Enin
Eyang nti

Names by Country/Language

Irish
Grand Mum
Maimeo
Mathair mhor
Mathar Chriona
Moria
Seanmhathair

Italian
Nonna
Nonnie
Nonnina

Japanese
Baachan
Obachan
Obaasan
Soba

Korean
Halmoni
Halmuhnee

Norwegian
Bestemor
Gammlemor
Oldemor

Phillipino
Lola
Nanay ng nanay

Polish
Babci
Babcia
Buscia

Portuguese
Avo
Vovo
Vovozinha

Romanian
Bunica
Mamaia
Tataia

Russian
Babushka
Buyukanne

Scottish
Bonnie My
Guid Mathair
Seanmhair

Serbian
Baba Deda
Mica

Spanish
Abuela
Abuelita
Lala Mamita
Vela

Swedish
Far-Mor
Mor-Mor
Phar-Mor

Taiwanese
Ama
Gua-ma

Turkish
Annanee
Babanne

Urkranian
Babusia

Vietmanese
Ba Na
Ba Ngoai

Yiddish
Bubbe
Bubby

PART V

**Grandmother
Names
by Personality**

Names by Personality Type

Cerebral
Beeta
Mae
Mica
Mummy
Tita
Wella

Energetic
Bibi
Birdie
Coco
Dodo
Galini
Lola

Stuffy
Binky
Bitsy
Contessa
Duchess
Fifi
Grand Meir

Classy
Didi
Gigi
Lady
Memere
Mimi
Vela

Fun
Beemie
Chickie
Gabby
Glamma
Goose
Jiggy

Romantic
Bella
Bubbles
Gaia
Goddess
Ona Great
Wella

Crafty
Bree
Golly
Gumma
Mummi
Ninna
Xena

Sporty
Cici
Gogo
Juju
Lilly
Moxiemom
Plucky

Traditional
Babka
Grammy
Grandma
Nana
Nonna
Oma

Domestic
Bana
Gada
Grossmutter
Ma
Marme
Tutu

Modern
Big Mama
Egge
Frannie
Gammommie
MeMom
Tootsie

Social
Dolly
Evie
Fancy
Ginny
Sugar
Sunny

To a small child, the perfect grand-dad is unafraid of big dogs and fierce storms but absolutely terrified of the word "boo."

—Robert Brault, Author

PART VI

The Best
Grandfather
Names

Abuelo (pronounced əbä-lō). Literally translated, "Grandfather." He has never colored his wavy salt and pepper hair.

Persona: Good-Looking Spanish Grandpa

Ace (pronounced ās). 1. A winning tennis serve. 2. Wears embarrassingly short, white tennis shorts.

Persona: Don't-Really-Care-What-I-Look-Like Grandpa

Fun Fact: The "Dream of Aces" card trick has become one of the most famous card tricks of all time.

Avo (pronounced āvō). Masculine, tough grandfather. Never took a hand-out once in his life.

Persona: Hard-Working Polish Grandpa

Baba (pronounced bä-bä). Can see all the magic and wonder of the world through his grandchildren's eyes.

Persona: Let's-Go-Build-a-Go-Cart Grandpa

Bear (pronounced bâr). Big, brawny on the outside, but soft on the inside.

Persona: Walks-Softly-but-Carries-a-Big-Stick Grandpa

Fun Fact: Chief Standing Bear was the famous and most feared chief of the Ponca Native Americans (1834-1908).

Big Daddy (pronounced bǐg dǎd-ē). His belly shakes when he laughs.

Persona: Larger-than-Life Grandpa

Bogey (pronounced bō-gē). 1. Golf term 2. He's always late for every family event.

Persona: Just-Let-Me-Finish-One-More-Thing Grandpa

Boss
(pronounced bôs). Watchful, judgmental grandfather.

Persona: Never-Misses-a-Move Grandpa

Fun Fact: The greedy, unethical commissioner on the TV sitcom, *Dukes of Hazzard*, was Boss Hogg.

Bub
(pronounced bŭb). He's a helpful grandfather.

Persona: Tinkering Grandpa

Fun Fact: The grandfather on the 1960s TV Sitcom *My Three Sons* was called Bub.

Bubba
(pronounced bŭb-bä). Loosely translated as *Good Ole Southern Boy.*

Persona: Soft-Southern-Drawl Grandpa

Fun Fact: Former President, Bill Clinton's childhood nickname was Bubba.

Buck
(pronounced bŭk). Old cowboy movies are an obsession with Buck, especially those starring actor John Wayne.

Persona: Cowboy Grandpa

Fun Fact: Buck Brannaman is the real-life "horse whisperer."

Bud
(pronounced bŭd). 1. Flower, blossom. 2. He enjoys Bud Light beer.

Persona: Party Grandpa

Fun Fact: Bud Light is the beer of choice for politically mainstream Americans.

Buddy
(pronounced bŭd-ē). He is your best friend.

Persona: Loyal Grandpa

Fun Fact: Buddy is the third most popular male dog name.

Buyukbaba
(pronounced bī-uk-bäbä). He is reserved and quiet. He likes to take long walks around town.

Persona: Nomadic Turkish Grandfather

Captain
(pronounced kăp-tən). 1. Commander of a ship. 2. Believes he is the commander of his home.

Persona: Supervisory Grandpa

Famous TV Actors: Captain Stubbing, Captain Kangaroo

Chief
(pronounced chēf). Like a fire chief, he is able to put out family fires quickly.

Persona: One-hot Grandpa

Fun Fact: The oldest firefighter in the U.S. is former Chief and current volunteer, Jack Lindsley, 98, of Lambertville, NJ.

Coach
(pronounced kōch). 1. Teacher, instructor. 2. Affable off the field; tyrannical on the field.

Persona: Every-Moment-Is-a-Teachable-Moment Grandpa

Famous Actor: Lovable Coach from TV sitcom *Cheers*.

Colonel
(pronounced kûr-nəl). 1. Military rank of a commissioned officer. 2. Proud to have served his country.

Persona: Chest-High-Shoulders-Back Grandpa

Fun Facts: Examples are Colonel Sanders of Kentucky Fried Chicken and Colonel Sherman Potter, MD, fictional character on *MASH*.

Crackers
(pronounced krăk-ərs). The years of nagging are starting to make him a bit "crackers."

Persona: Hanging-in-There Grandpa

Dad-Dad (pronounced dăd-dăd). Enjoys a cold beer after mowing the lawn.

Persona: Double-Trouble Grandpa

Dedyshka (pronounced děd-ĭsh-kä). Loves big family gatherings.

Persona: Big Russian Grandpa

Doc (pronounced dŏc). Able to solve all problems.

Persona: Comforting Grandpa

Famous TV Doctors: Marcus Welby, Hawkeye Pierce, Doogie Howser, Cliff Huxtable and gunslinger, Doc Holiday.

Duke (pronounced dōōk). 1. A nobleman with the highest hereditary rank. 2. Very proud of his ancestry and offspring.

Persona: Handsome English Grandpa

Farfar (pronounced fär-fär). Literally translated as Father's Father.

Persona: Fair-Skinned Dutch Grandpa

Fun Fact: Vincent van Gogh was a famous Dutch Post-Impressionist painter. He lived 1853-1890.

Fly (pronounced flī). Literally translated as "to engage in flight." He never stays in one place for very long.

Persona: On-the-Fly Grandpa

Fun Fact: Fly fishing is growing in popularity with the ladies.

Glampa   (pronounced glăm-pä). His classic good looks and strong physique make him seem like a movie star.

Persona: Hollywood Grandpa

G-Pa   (pronounced jē-pä). An instigator who loves riling up the grandchildren.

Persona: Crazy Grandpa

Godfather   (pronounced gŏd-fä-thər). If you look like Marlon Brando and have a family business…then Godfather it is.

Persona: Dark-Suit-Wearing Italian Grandpa

Fun Fact: *The Godfather* movies depict the fictitious Corleone crime family in the 1920s. Marlon Brando won an Oscar for his portrayal of Don Corleone, the Godfather.

Gramps   (pronounced grămps). Informal name for Grandfather.

Persona: Nice Grandpa

Famous TV Actors: The Grandfather on the 1970s TV show, *Lassie*, was called Gramps.

Grampy   (pronounced grăm-pē). Can always fix a broken bike.

Persona: Just-Let-Me-Take-a-Look-Here Grandpa

Grandad   (pronounced grăn-dăd). He has not missed a Sunday church sermon in over 40 years.

Persona: Good-Ole-Religious Grandpa

Grandfather   (pronounced grănd-fä-thər). He is somewhat stand-offish around small children.

Persona: Walks-Slowly Grandpa

Quote: Bill Cosby's Grandfather used to say, "Don't worry about senility. When it hits you, you won't know it."

Grandpa   (pronounced grănd-pä). Easy-going and likeable.

Persona: Just-Call-Me Grandpa

Fun Fact: Grandpa Munster, from the 1960s TV sit-com, *The Munsters*, could turn himself into a bat.

Grandpapa   (pronounced grănd-päpä). Studied marine biology in college and now enjoys taking the grandkids to the beach.

Persona: Not-Afraid-to-Swim-with-the-Sharks Grandpa

Famous: One of the most famous sea explorers in the world, Jacques Cousteau, is called Grandpapa.

Grandpaw   (pronounced grănd-pô). With his deep southern drawl, he can capture an audience with his raucous boyhood stories.

Persona: Deep-South Grandpa

Grandpee   (pronounced grăn-pē). No matter how many designer shirts or pants he is given, he never fails to look unfashionable.

Persona: Fashion-Isn't-His-Thing Grandpa

Grootvader   (pronounced grōōt-väd-ər). Passionate about brewing his own signature beer in the garage.

Persona: Gotta-Have-a-Hobby German Grandpa

Fun Fact: Until 1988, in adherence to the Reinheitsgebot, German beer-making only allowed water, hops and malt as ingredients. Wheat beer had to be top-fermented.

Grootvater   (pronounced grōōt-vät-ər). Big, sturdy and surprisingly open-minded.

Persona: Fair-and-Impartial Dutch Grandpa

Grumpa   (pronounced grŭm-pä). Worries about the stock market daily.

Persona: Financial Grandpa

Grumpy   (pronounced grŭm-pē). Does not like it when family events are scheduled during football season.

Persona: Former-High-School-Football-Athlete Grandpa

Halaboji   (pronounced hăl-ä-bŭ-jē). Chooses his words carefully.

Persona: Man-of-Few-Words Korean Grandpa

Itsy   (pronounced ĭt-sē). One who is willing to see the big picture. He does not sweat the small stuff like losing his keys and glasses daily.

Persona: Optimistic Grandpa

Jumpy

(**pronounced jŭm-pē**). Jumpy takes a little something before the grandchildren come over.

Persona: Likes-It-on-the-Quiet-Side Grandpa

King

(**pronounced kĭng**). Thinks he is King of the castle.

Persona: High-and-Mighty Grandpa

Fun Fact: The tomb of King Tut, the Egyptian pharaoh, was discovered in 1922. Over 3,000 years old, the tomb contained golden riches.

Lito

(**pronounced lē-tō**). His handle-bar mustache is starting to grey.

Persona: Mustache-Twisting Spanish Grandpa

Lolo

(**pronounced lō-lō**). Can float in the ocean for hours.

Persona: Light-as-a-Feather Philippines Grandpa

Lumpy

(**pronounced lŭm-pē**). Too many nights spent watching TV has made Grampa a bit "lumpy."

Persona: Late-Night-TV Grandpa

Mate

(**pronounced māt**). Still adores his Mate after all these years.

Persona: He-Only-Has-Eyes-For-Her Grandpa

Mepaw

(**pronounced mē-pä**). Loose southern translation, "My Father."

Persona: Can-Still-Drive-that-John-Deere-Tractor Grandpa

Morfar
(pronounced mōr-fär). Literally translated as Mother's Father.

Persona: Blonde-Headed Swedish Grandpa

Fun Fact: In Sweden, you can take sick leave during your vacation if you fall ill.

Nonno
(pronounced nŏn-nō). He claims his "meat-a-balls" have no competition. They are the world's best.

Persona: Apron-Wearing Italian Grandpa

Fun Fact: Nonni's Italian Eatery (N.H.) created the world's largest, edible meatball in 2009. It weighed 222.5 pounds and was certified by Guinness Book of World Records.

Oji-chan
(pronounced oji-chän). Drives very slowly and carefully.

Persona: Takes-One-Day-at-a-Time Japanese Grandpa

Opa
(pronounced ō-pä). Card tricks and board games are his specialty.

Persona: Fun German Grandpa

Pa
(pronounced pä). Likes to wear his old, broken-in cowboy hat. He has been wearing it so long he feels naked without it.

Persona: Habitual Grandpa

Papa
(pronounced pä-pä). You always feel safe and loved when you are with Papa.

Persona: Best-Kind-Of Grandpa

Papaw　(pronounced pä-pô). Willing to teach each of his grandchildren how to duck hunt.

Persona: Loaded-Gun Grandpa

Fun Fact: Geocaching is a new treasure hunting game. GPS is used to hide and seek containers with other participants in the activity. www.Geocaching.com

Papoo　(pronounced pă-pōō). His RV displays all the campgrounds they have visited.

Persona: Enjoying-Retired-Life Grandpa

Pappous　(pronounced pă-pōōs). Will drive over an hour to his favorite Greek restaurant.

Persona: Loves-His-Old-Country Greek Grandpa

Fun Fact: An "Eggoni" is a grandchild of Pappous.

Papi　(pronounced păp-pē). He's one happy Papi.

Persona: Always-in-High-Spirits Grandpa

Fun Fact: "Big Papi" is the designated baseball hitter for the Boston Red Sox. His hits helped the team win their 2004 and 2007 World Series Championships.

Paw　(pronounced pôw). His family has been growing tobacco for generations.

Persona: Got-a-Light Grandpa

Pepere　(pronounced pĕp-âr). Bow-tie wearing grandfather.

Persona: Serious French Grandpa

Pickles (pronounced pĭk-əls). At any time, he can be either slick, prickly or very sour.

Persona: Hard-to-Understand Grandpa

Fun Quote: "Hunger is the best pickle." —*Ben Franklin*

Pilot (pronounced pī-lət). He is easy-going and takes care of himself.

Persona: Willing-to-Try-New-Things Grandpa

Pop (pronounced pŏp). Always has change in his pocket for the ice cream truck.

Persona: Habit-of-Jiggling-the-Coins-in-His-Pocket Grandpa

Poppi (pronounced pŏp-pē). He is handy around the house and yard.

Persona: Tool-Belt-Wearing Grandpa

Fun Fact: Poppy seed is an oilseed obtained from the opium poppy.

Pop-Pop (pronounced pŏp-pŏp). He is a grandpa who is twice the fun.

Persona: Popular Grandpa

Puff (pronounced pŭff). He is just like a cream puff. Hard on the outside, but soft on the inside.

Persona: Old-Softy Grandpa

Picky

(pronounced pĭk-ēē). Bought the grandkids a karaoke machine so he could practice with them.

Persona: Whistles-While-He-Works Grandpa

Fun Facts: The 1970s hit comedy TV show, *I Love Lucy*, Desi Arnaz played husband Ricky, who was a night-club owner, singer and bandleader.

Seanathair

(pronounced shăn-a-hər). Still has all his freckles and boyish good looks.

Persona: Irish Grandpa

Skipper

(pronounced skĭp-ər). He is good at bossing under-lings around.

Persona: Seafaring Grandpa

Famous TV Actors: The Skipper was the captain of the S.S. Minnow and leader on 1960s *Gilligan's Island* TV show.

Sonny

(pronounced sŭn-ē). He is someone who has had many different and interesting careers.

Persona: Sweet-Singing Grandpa

Fun Facts: Sonny & Cher (Bono) were an American pop music duo and entertainers in the 1970s. Sonny Bono was a singer, entertainer, actor, record producer and politician.

Sumo

(pronounced sōō-mō). He has a very slow, but delib-erate gait.

Persona: Short and Thick Grandpa

Fun Fact: Sumo is a stylized form of Japanese wrestling.

Tiger
(pronounced tī-gər). He greets you with gentle jabs and punches.

Persona: Pretend-Boxer Grandpa

Tutu Kane
(pronounced tōō-tōō-kān). He has a peaceful and calm spirit.

Persona: Aloha-Spirit Hawaiian Grandpa

Ye-Ye
(pronounced yē-yē). Faithfully does his chores every day.

Persona: Hard-Working-til-the-End Chinese Grandpa

Zayde
(pronounced zā-dē). Happy and willing to take direction from Bubbe. He likes to keep the peace.

Persona: Peace-Maker Jewish Grandpa

Zsa-Zsa
(pronounce zä-zä). His grandchildren are in awe of his long fluffy white beard.

Persona: Santa-Claus-Look-Alike Polish Grandpa

PART VII
Perfect Pairs:
Names that Go Together Perfectly

Perfect Pairs

Airy — Ace

Bebe — Bear

Birdie — Bogey

Bitsy — Itsy

Bossie — Boss

Bubbe — Zayde

Chickie — Farfar

Chickie — Coach

Coco — Puff

Cici — Captain

Dame — Duke

Didi — Baba

Ditti — Doc

Duchess — Duke

Gigi — Gramps

Gigi — Poppi

Glamma — Glampa

Granny — Grampy

Gram — Crackers

Happy — Grumpy

Huggie — Bear

Indy — Chief

Jumpy — Lumpy

Juno — Jupiter

Lolly — Pop

Lucy — Ricky

MeMaw — MePaw

Mimi — Ace

Mimi — Mate

MopMop — PopPop

Nana — Papa

Nanoo — Papoo

Queenie — Ace

Queenie — King

Sassy — Pappy

Sugar — Big Daddy

Tickles — Pickles

YaYa — PaPa

"Enjoy the little things, for one day you may look back and realize they were the big things."

—Robert Brault, Author

Made in the USA
Middletown, DE
03 December 2019